W8

Mahatma Gandhi said: "There are many ways to truth and each of us sees truth in fragment." The seeker after truth or beauty is conditioned by his own desire as well as by his background and experience.

These photographs are beautiful. Yet they can give a glimpse of only a part of India's infinite variety. India is ever changing and renewing herself. Today she is consciously and determinedly struggling with many old problems, and meeting the challenge of new ones.

Our modernization cannot be an aping of the West. It must be according to our own needs and in the light of our great heritage. Thus, even as we develop and change, we shall remain different, we shall retain our distinct individuality and so perhaps, those who view life only from a particular angle, may find us difficult to comprehend.

Madame Renou's introduction is both scholarly and sensitive and reveals a rare understanding of India's continuing endeavour to find "harmony between the inner man and his ever-changing outer environment".

(Indira Gandhi)

New Delhi,
September 19, 1968.

MY INDIA

I am not a specialist on Indian matters. The reader will find no erudition displayed here. Before the world of thought which is India one can only sense his own ignorance. But I love her, and however insufficiently I know her, I write these pages only to pay my debt to her.

In the nineteenth century, when the "European fatherland" was beginning to take root, Michelet dreamed of a *Banquet of Sufficient Life* for all men and asked himself what each European nation had given to him and what he owed it. "Quid retribuam vobis?" he asked, *"my* Germany, *my* England... *my* Italy." It is in this same spirit that I write today. We are not even yet the "good Europeans" we were supposed to be, and yet who doesn't sense that time is already urging us to become citizens of the world if we do not want soon to be more lived than living? It is not through any heartfelt generosity that, according to the ancient words of the Latin poet, nothing human is foreign to us. We cannot open a newspaper without feeling a sort of dependence on and responsibility for everything going on in the world. It has never been more urgent to work to assure all men of *a sufficient life,* and we must cure the hunger of others if we wish to be sure of our own lives. "My America" (Emerson, Thoreau, Whitman, Wilson), "My Russia" (Tolstoi, Dostoevski, Gorki, Pasternak)—I know very well what I owe them. Michelet said that, owing to their diversity, each of the great nations is a lesson, an "education", for all the others. "My India?" I am well aware of all she has taught me in fifty years, of exactly what my debt is to certain encounters, to some of its *gurus,* to Tagore, to Gandhi, to Nehru.

The first Hindus I saw were soldiers. It was in 1915. I had been wounded. In the hospital in a small village in Flanders, I could watch from my bed the constant flow of men, the youth of the world who seemed to have agreed to meet here to nourish the war and to die together. There were French, English, Canadians, Australians, Senegalese, every color, every race. And then one morning, I remember, there were Hindu warriors, Sikhs. Sitting in fronts of small carts they urged their animals on with long sticks. They were handsome. Their eyes shone like black diamonds. It seemed to me they looked like princes of wisdom when, in reality, they were only, like the rest of us, unskilled laborers. They were fighting the war with us, for us, having come from far, far away. Why? How could this be? Their presence did little to answer the many questions I began to ask myself. That I should be there could be explained by good or bad reasons: the old European disorder, the confused and endless history of the boundaries around our small fields. But they? Was our disorder contagious and was the absurd, by their presence, proving itself? I forgot about them. I was sent behind the lines, having fallen ill, and consequently, according to the logic of the time, unfit to be killed and to die. However, a few months later I came in contact with Tagore. I had been assigned as an interpreter in Lyon in a postal censor service, whose duty it was to control all correspondence between the world and Switzerland. And thus one day I came across a small green booklet which had come straight from Japan: it was the text of an admirable lecture given by Rabindranath Tagore in

Japan, a "Message from India to Japan." This message, joined by other essays, later became a complete book which I succeeded in obtaining: *Nationalism.* This book opened a debate for me which has not ceased in fifty years.

I scarcely knew the name of the poet. I had read in 1913 the translation that André Gide had published of the *Gitanjali* but found only a literary interest in it. Let's admit it: we know very little about the Orient, that whole world which seems to be lying outside Europe's backdoor. All the traditions of our culture had comfortably attached us to the small Mediterranean pond. Undoubtedly the true benefit that we obtained from our immense misfortunes was the occasion they gave us to recognize our brothers everywhere, brothers who were often more attentive and lucid about ourselves than we were. The moral lesson in *Gitanjali* suddenly took on a much broader sense. That hymn to inner life naturally ended in the lyrical pamphlet *Nationalism,* in the greatest condemnation yet made of the mad aberration of Western civilization: war. All the poet's cries spoke to my heart, and even the grandeur of the lament was a comfort to me.

The war, he explained, was the fatal issue of the ambitions and inhuman political policies of the West. The ethics of power "dehumanizes" man, and if it becomes the official ethics, the national ethics, if it recruits from a whole nation an anonymous and untold force, then its power is evil and limitless. Then a nation is only an organization, an administration, a factory, a warehouse, an army. It's only concern is maximum efficiency; it reduces as much as possible the personal life of man; it develops only his professional life. Men, according to its reckoning, cease to be men, living souls, to become no more than manpower or soldiers. This "dehumanization" took place over the course of a century. And, the poet cries out, *"This European war is a war of atonement. Man, the moral being, should protest in the name of his very life against the accumulation of things in which the heart should have its say, against systems and politics in which the living human fraternity cannot exist. The time has come when, for the salvation of the whole outraged world, Europe must fully acknowledge the terrible absurdity of this thing called the Nation."* This small book began to help me to live, inspiring me by a great example, and as only the words of Romain Rolland had previously done, to think what I thought. All the newspapers of the world were predicting the end of Europe. A large number of my friends were dead. My doubts increased daily over the legitimacy of such a hideous slaughter. And chance put between my hands those pages which were the most comprehensive commentary on the European drama and the most moving call to universal fraternity. Was there a tinge of resentment in those words, the legitimate rancor of a world colonized by a Western nation? No, Tagore was speaking of something beyond the Hindu nation itself. He could not even conceive of a power that could wish to submit to that sort of mechanization, which was the very essence of nationalism. I admired that denunciation of the European will to power. I must admit that I regretted, nonetheless, that he did not recognize more explicitly the part that the will to enlighten played in European activities. No, I could not believe, even at the height of the war, that we were dehumanized to such a degree. The advocation of an inner life only had its perils, its hypocrisies, especially when the rich took it upon themselves to edify the poor. We, in Europe, were more materialistic and there was something to be said for that. It is not enough, alas, to deny or despise the power of materialism to destroy it. Futher-

8

more, I seemed to discover occasionally in Tagore's thinking a European accent. I desired for "my France" just exactly what he desired for his own country when he wrote:

> *There where the spirit is without fear and where one can hold his head high,*
> *There where knowledge is free,*
> *There where the world has not been shattered by narrow domestic walls,*
> *Where words spring from the profoundest truth,*
> *Where tireless effort reaches for perfection,*
> *Where the clear river of reason has not lost its way among the dreary sands of dead habits,*
> *Where the spirit always goes on ahead, led by you, to an ever larger thought and activity,*
> *Under this sky of freedom, my Father, make my country awaken!*

I seemed to hear in these verses the common hope of men reconciled at last.

★

It was thanks to Romain Rolland that I was able to follow life in India for years. He had become my friend. No Frenchman has had a closer, more continuous relationship with India during the period between the two wars. Thanks to him I was able to follow Gandhi's struggle for the independence of his country. His *Diary* is undoubtedly the most fascinating account of it that exists. I recommend it to my readers (1).

---

(1) Romain Rolland. *Inde.* Journal 1915-1943. Ed. Albin-Michel.

What a strange and marvelous combat, one that was fought with only one arm—the refusal to have recourse to arms, the *ahimsa,* non-violence, the power of truth, the *satiagraha;* the profound conviction and the willingness to die for it, if necessary, that nothing can weaken—even the force of a whole empire—the consciousness and radiation, throughout a whole nation, of the justice and truth it carries within itself! What a surprise in this world of force, where war and the European revolution had imprisoned us! What a remarkable example and what a proposition for reflection! What a language for a new form of revolution! I read his journal, *Young India,* the letters to the disciples in his hermitage, his *Ashram,* which he often sent them from prison. I can only cite here a few phrases from those extraordinary messages, and propose them to my readers as food for thought;

> *It requires rather arduous training to reach a mental state of non-violence.*
> *I have found it impossible to alleviate the suffering of the wretched by singing them a song from Kabir. The starving masses demand only one poem: comforting nourishment. It should not be given to them as charity. They must earn it. Now they can only earn it by the sweat of their brow.*
> *I would rather be torn to shreds than not recognize my brothers in the repressed classes... I do not wish to be born again, but if I am I would like to be reborn among the Untouchables in order to share their affronts and to work for their liberation.*
> *Non-violence is not benevolent submission to the evil-doer. Non-violence opposes all the strength of the soul to the will of the tyrant. One man can thus defy an empire and bring about its fall.*

What strict discipline is required for that non-violence, that active resistance! I don't know if there is a more extraordinary act in Gandhi's life than a decision he made in 1922: he had taught the masses to practice civil discipline so effectively that the Prince of Wales, visiting Calcutta on December 24, 1922, crossed a deserted city. Men and woman everywhere were volunteeering to go to prison. However, a few weeks later a demonstration in Chauri-Chaura turned out badly: the police attacked the mob and the latter set fire to the central police station and massacred all of them. Gandhi then suspended his order for "civil disobedience" and inflicted a five-day fast on himself. *"I must submit,"* he wrote, *"to a personal purification. I must be in a state to sense more acutely the slightest variation in the morale of the people... Each time they commit errors I will continue to plead guilty for them. The only tyrant that I accept on this earth is the 'small silent voice'."* History has had its great moments. By such strange battles India won its liberty. I saw Gandhi only once. It was in 1931, during his European trip. He spoke in Paris at the Magic City. Truth emanated from his slender, humble person. He explained the arm of peace, which alone could change life and the world *"Everything,"* he told us, *"should be done openly and without recourse to war. Truth hates secrecy. The more openly you act, the more chance you have of remaining truthful."*

★

I met Jawaharlal Nehru twice. The first time was in 1935. A young Hindu writer, Raja Rao, invited me to lunch with Nehru when he was in Paris. I knew a great deal about this silent man on the other side of the table. He was a revolutionary leader. He had been fighting for

11

his people for sixteen years. He had been imprisoned frequently and for long periods. He was married, he had a small daughter, Indira. He had employed the time spent in prison writing a world history for her. He was passing through Paris because his wife was seriously ill in a sanatorium in Switzerland, and English justice had suddenly freed him from the Almora prison so that he could go to her, but it was on the condition that he would not return to India before the expiration of his prison term. Everything about the man impressed me, and I scarcely spoke.

I met him again in New Delhi, in 1961. He was now the chief of State, the *guru* of the entire nation. I had only a morning left to spend in India. He had just returned from the United States the day before, sick, exhausted. He wanted to see me before my departure. I was touched by so much kindness. I spent that entire last morning with him. I gave him an account of my impressions of the Tagore seminar, which I had just attended as the French representative. The debates had been impassioned. To discuss them as I did, was, at the same time, to ask him all the questions that preoccupied both of us: the future of our world, the role of our Western societies of consumers, of Communism, of India. I had been told that he had great powers of concentration. I learned that he was not at all afraid of silences, those silences that bother our Western loquacity. Perhaps this came from his imprisonments. I questioned him. He reflected, answered slowly and gravely. I got the impression that he was, in his international action, more influenced by Tagore's spirit than by Gandhi's. When I remarked that one of the greatest absurdities of our time seemed to me to be that those two antagonistic worlds, those two systems, the American and the Soviet, which at any moment could plunge us into war, were nonetheless basically alike if, in the name of different ideologies, with their all-enveloping conformisms, they were attempting to manufacture the same poor conformist and subjugated man, I saw a spark of malice in his eyes:

"Those two worlds," he said, "both want very much to be loved!" He did not add that this was asking a lot but I sensed that he thought so. I laughed. I had not thought of this similarity between the two. But I cannot recount here all of our conversation. In this man the wisdom of the West and the Orient were so strangely interwoven that, in his own words, he experienced a spiritual solitude. *"I am a stranger in the West,"* he wrote, *"I cannot be part of it, but in my own country, too, I sometimes feel exiled."* It is undoubtedly for that very reason that he could do our world so much good. I have reread the letters he wrote from prison in 1933 to his young daughter Indira, who is now, in her turn, at the head of her country. The last letter is full of greatness. He was going to be freed. He had cited in his letter several poems, one in French by Verlaine, of whom he was reminded by the sound of the rain falling on the roof of his cell: "Oh, the gentle sound of rain..." Then suddenly: *"I am going to end,"* he wrote, *"with one more quotation. It is a poem from the* Gitanjali, *a poem or a prayer by Rabindranath Tagore."* And it was the same poem that I quoted earlier:

> *"There where the spirit is without fear...*
>
> . . . .
>
> *... make my country awaken!"*

The India of which he dreamed and which he made, like that of Tagore, belongs to the world.

Jean Guéhenno

Marie-Simone RENOU.

In memory of my husband.

I want, for the morning song,
to magnifiy the Dawn and Night...
(Hymn from the Rig-Véda.)

Since my earliest childhood I have had a desire to know India. A vague, misty desire, scarcely supported by the clouds of the marvelous, so floating that it asked nothing of reality and could not be disappointed by it.

Later I went there, not to satisfy a simple curiosity one has about a different civilization, but as a sort of passionate rendezvous with another world.

Besides, who can escape its fascination?

It insinuates itself into our dreams in a thousand different ways. For some, the door is opened by Kipling and Kim's long travels through northern India. For others, by the poems of Tagore. It exports fakirs who disconcert by inexplicable magic, and yogis who give a foretaste of what spiritual powers can be. Its art, in turn serene, tumultuous, descriptive or superlatively monumental, astounds us. And we experience a thirst for its Wisdom.

To go to India, one should take the old terrestial route which passes through the gorges that led to Taxila from ancient Bactria, one of the principal crossroads of the ancient world.

"Source of happiness or misfortune for India?" This road was the first one used by the Aryan invaders in the second millenary B.C. They thrust forward in the direction of the Indus, from the Oxus River, now called Amu Darya, the present northern border of Aghanistan.

Much later, Cyrus and Darius' Persians, Alexander's Greeks and their successors, the Scythians, the Parthians, the Tokharians, the Huns, the Turks, the Arabs, the Mongolians, used this wide road which led most easily from the fertile plains of Bactria to those of Hindustan. In all ages "missionaries, merchants, artists, doctors, astrologers, mountebanks, adventurers" traveled over it in caravans. Leaving in early autumn, the season "when there is the least snow on the ground, the least water in the torrents and the fewest storms in the sky," climbing the high passes, following the narrow trails, slipping between red sandstone, winding around the dunes in the middle of the desert, crossing the plains, they reached Und, not far from Taxila, the "Door of India."

It was very near there that Alexander crossed the Indus on a bridge of ships prepared by his lieutenants.

It was there also that the Chinese pilgrim Hiuan-Tsang, in the 7th century A.D., crossed by boat from one bank to the other to call on the Emperor Harshavardhana, the man who regrouped the northern provinces after the collapse of the Gupta empire, and creator of the last pre-Mussulman empire of India. After becoming the confident and friend of the prince, he wrote a chronicle of his reign and then departed by the same traditional passageway, but on the back of an elephant this time, taking advantage of the low water of winter.

Like the pilgrims of the Middle Ages, making their way to Saint-Jacques-de-Compostelle, one could dream of taking this slow approach, mixing with the crowd of travelers. Afterwards, caravaneers charted their course by the stars when the trail was wiped out by wind storms, winding around such huge mountain masses that, accord-

The temple of Cidambaram symbolizes the center of the universe and at the same time the concept of Being. It was here that Siva-Nataraja performed the cosmic dance Nadanta. *"Our god Siva is the dancer like unto the latent heat in wood, who diffuses his power in matter and the spirit and makes them dance too."* The *faithful worship and venerate the "God of the Dance"* in this immense temple in *proportion to the mystic dance which animates worlds.*

ing to a thousand-year-old legend, "even the birds could not pass over them except on foot!" And, camping at each of the fifty or sixty stops which marked out at intervals of fifteen to eighteen miles the way to the Promised Land, one learned such ancient oral traditions that they seemed to have inspired the oldest literary texts.

The immense trapezium which constitutes Hindustan opens up only after Peshawar. It is closed in the north and more or less isolated from the rest of the land by the highest rampart in the world: the Himalayas, which can even arrest the passage of the monsoon clouds. After the fertile Indo-Gangetic plain, parallel with and south of the Tropic of Cancer, the base of the triangle is formed by the Deccan. The eastern and western coasts of the Indian Ocean, from the Gulf of Cambay and the Gulf of Bengal, move towards the south, growing closer and finally joining to form the tip of Cape Cormorin.

★

The excessive is common measure in India. Today it numbers 510 million inhabitants. There were 410 million in 1958!

But these people do not all belong to the same race. They differ in height, from tall to medium; in facial features, from fine to rather coarse; and in color of eyes, from the very deepest brown to light brown. It is even possible, although very exceptional, to find gray or blue.

The color of their skin varies from slightly white to a pronounced swarthiness in the northern populations, to varying shades of yellow in the east; it becomes black in the south, but Indian black, topped by wavy or curly hair.

All variations of intermediary types, not only from

Not far from the Sun Temple of Modhera and the riotous overloading of its medieval decoration, a pilgrim stops to rest. He has chosen the reposing simplicity of this classic post-Gupta architecture.

These capriciously sha[ped]
temples, crowded toget[her]
cover Mount Catrunj[a]
like a prayer man[tra].
More than 900 of th[em]
are found here in Pa[li-]
tana, in northwest[ern]
India, the most popu[lar]
of Jainist holy pla[ces].
In the 11th century [a]
rich merchant in [the]
community transform[ed]
two hills into a si[ngle]
mountain by filling [in]
the depression betw[een]
them. Temples of w[hite]
marble connected by m[azes]
of galleries and punctua[ted]
by sanctuary towers w[ere]
then built. Far from h[ere,]
in Madura, in south[ern]
India, from the top [of]
each gopura of [the]
temple-city of Minak[shi]
one can view the ensem[ble]
of buildings. The relig[ious]
scenes described by [the]
reliefs in terra cotta on [the]
superstructure, appear, [to]
the eyes of the devout, [to]
be alive through the m[agic]
of bright paints [that]
periodically revive th[em].

one province to the next, but even within the same groups, complicates the classifications one attempts to establish.

Yet it is impossible to confuse Indians with foreigners in their country. However dissimilar they may be among themselves, they appear to be marked by a mysterious sign that proves their Indian origin "for there are Indian manners of wearing an Iranian or Mongolian face!"

Furthermore, the extraordinary variety of spoken languages does not always coincide with racial characteristics.

Before the two vast enclaves which, with a population today of 108 million inhabitants, constitutes the Mussulman Republic of Pakistan, were detached from India in 1947, the Linguistic Office of the Indian Government counted 179 languages, to which were added 544 dialects. Today the Indian Constitution officially recognizes fourteen, headed by Hindu, which was made the national tongue.

If one excludes the Himalayan dialects and those of unevolved tribes, the languages of India are connected in the north with the Indo-Aryan group, and are derived from Sanskrit. In the south they are associated with Dravidian, and are dominated by a language of great culture: Tamil. It is very difficult to diffuse throughout India a knowledge of Hindu, with its structure so different from that of Dravidian, so English retains the advantage of being understood, not by all, but by a large number throughout the entire territory. Thus English is maintained, despite a national desire to make it disappear from the list of official languages and although it is not anyone's "mother tongue."

★

The graceful pyramids of the Mavali puram temple serve as a landmark for navigators. For thirteen centuries, since the reigns of the kings Pallava Narashimhavaram II and Rajasimha, the sea has pounded the granite, and the monsoon winds have gnawed away at the delicately decorated roofs. For a very long time now foreign sailors have not anchored on this shore, but innumerable tourists enliven the site. These fishermen's wives, indifferent to the beauty of the landscape, gather shells tossed ashore by the sea and will use them to make charming multicolored necklaces.

December the fields are covered with luxuriant crops; the southern Indian peasants quickly reap this golden harvest to prepare the rice fields. ...fore the second sowing, this young boy, mounted on a swing-plow, flattens the earth and guides his team of black water buffaloes straight towards ...East and urges them on in a splattering of mud. The sight of garnered rice warms the hearts of the peasants and their wives who tend the ...ldren. Around the houses of the village, bushes and vines are covered with fragrant flowers, and soon the coconut trees will bend under the weight ...ripe fruit. In love with stone as the peasant is with grain, the village stonecutter sculptures idols destined to be placed throughout the country, ...ng the roads and in the temples.

Land of oral tradition, India, by means of professional reciters, has transmitted from generation to generation and over long centuries its first literary works before they were ever written down.

This might explain its scorn for chronology. Why record the birth of a written text that has been so long interwoven with the thought that formed it?

Nonetheless, the most ancient documents can be traced back to the second millenary B.C., when the Aryan tribes "invaded Northwest India, bringing with them the rudiments of the Vedic religion." Inspired and led by their national god Indra, who encourages their exploits, they sing their requests to him:

"Endow our bodies with strength, O Indra,
  strength for our beasts of burden,
  strength for our children and our descendants
  so they may live!
  For you are the giver of strength."

And they ask for his intervention:

"O Indra, with your abundant help,
  the best possible,
  invigorate us today, O generous one, O hero!
  He who wishes us evil, make him fall lower,
  and he whom we wish evil to befall,
  may the breath of life abandon him!"

In existence two thousand years before the birth of Christ, these hymns seem to be examples of a very archaic language called Vedic, but which was already Sanskrit. At about the time of the Christian era it attained its classical form, and, always receptive to new

"City of temples", Palitana welcomes constant pilgramages. Here the Jains venerate the 24 Tirthankaras, "the ferrymen," or "announcers of salvation," the last of whom was Mahariva, or Jina, the founder of their religion.

domains of expression, it developed without a break up to our time. Thus it can be said that without doubt no other literature equals that of Sanskrit in shear bulk or can match the length of the time-span during which it was cultivated.

It reflects the whole of Indian civilization, steeped in religious inspirations, even in theatrical expression, in lyrical and in technical fields.

As for the great epic poem, it emanates from beliefs, "illustrates and popularizes them." It is presented in the form of two immense poetic collections: *Mahabharata* and the *Ramayana,* composed between the three centuries preceding and the three centuries following the beginning of the Christian era.

The *Mahabharata* contains almost 100,000 couplets; the subject is borrowed from the heroic legend *The Great Bharata (Story of War).* Symbol of the struggle between Good and Evil, it recounts the inexorable rivalry between the two branches of the descendants of Bharata. A tremendous war, in which tribes from all over India and neighboring countries participated, opposing the one hundred Kuaravas and their cruel chief to the five Pandava brothers, allies of the god Krishna. For eighteen days the battle raged with such violence that the heavens disappeared, as if veiled by flying arrows. The dead accumulated, the Kuaravas leaders perished one after another. However, one escaped and reached "the fearsome forest full of trees and vines of all sorts." There, "consumed by anger, he could not sleep" and sought a means of revenge.

"The powerful warrior looked around the forest... and as he was looking at these wooded places, haunted by beasts... he saw birds perched on a banyan. They were crows, thousands of them, who were spending the

Sprawling over almost a mile, a triple quadrilateral of galleries, broken by transversal corridors, forms an enclosure around the sanctuary where the heart of the Rameshvaram temple beats. The edifice rests on enormous granite pillars: like our medieval cathedrals, it remains a witness to a collective faith, to the fervor of an anonymous multitude—foremen, laborers and sculptors. Nothing has changed in four centuries: cool semi-darkness, streams of light falling at regular intervals through lateral openings, white phantoms of women draped in saris. A labyrinth, undoubtedly, but where a bewildered neophyte will always find a faithful one to guide his steps.

Hands joined, the devout murmur their prayer—the mantra, which has the magic power of speech—and place offerings at the divinities' feet. One offers what one likes best: buttermilk, garlands of flowers; Siva receives blue corollas, and Vishnu white jasmine. The oblation of fire, agnihotra, is one of the most important ceremonies. It includes gestures, rhythmical chants and perfume: thus the pious man is carried away towards a divine world.

night... However, while the crows were sleeping in complete confidence, he suddenly saw an owl arrive, terrible to see, with its deep cry, its large body and yellow eyes, its long beak and claws; reddish brown, as rapid as an eagle.

"Softening his voice, like a slithering serpent, he headed for a branch of the banyan. Diving at the branch, the winged beast killed, en masse, the birds sleeping there: he was the birds' Death. He cut off the wings of some, crushed heads, or, using his claws as a weapon, broke their legs. In an instant the vigorous bird killed all those within his range, and around the banyan was a circle of dismembered bodies. The owl was full of joy at having killed the crows: he was glutted with revenge, the slaughterer of his enemies."

Then the fierce warrior said to himself:

"This bird has taught me a lesson for my combat. The time has come for me to destroy my enemies."

And while they slept he carried out a horrible slaughter of the Pandavas' allies.

The five brothers escaped and completed their earthly mission until the eldest ascended to heaven.

An epic with a sad ending but softened by the Indian notion of destiny. The *Mahabharata,* one of the great sources of Hinduism, is an account of its beliefs.

It is, above all, a verse-chronicle of Krishna, the real leader in battles, the incarnation of the god Vichnu, whose divine nature reveals itself in magisterial interventions.

Far from being only a long tale expressing with artful vigor the somber grandeur of war, there are also episodes

In big, gleaming copper pots, in dull pewter or in pottery, the women will solemnly carry back on their head or hip their provisions of water. During the period of gossip by the fountain, local news is exchanged. Formerly, each social group had its own fountain, but this problem is now resolved: "a well has a caste," a proverb says, "a faucet does not."

In Çringeri, in the Mai-
sura region, her offering
accomplished, transformed by
the nearness of the divinity,
a woman leaves the temple
protected by two stone guardians and returns to the
world. The temples of
Mount Abu are examples
of India's medieval "baro-
que." An amazing technical
feat of stonecutting surround-
ing the divinity has endowed
him with a dynamic attitude.

full of charm, interposed as a form of digression. Damayanti's devotion, tinged with ingenious fidelity, succeeds in saving her husband, King Nala, from the demon of gambling. The moving love of Savitri persuades the god of death to give back her husband.

But the most admirable of all the passages, and also the best known, is the *Bhagavad-Gita,* the "Song of the Blessed One". In it, Krishna, revealing himself as the Bhagavant, "Supreme Lord", destroys the hero Arjuna's fear at the moment of going into combat. He teaches him the act without desire, leading to Deliverance by the way of the *Bhakti,* the way of ardent love, of union with the Blessed One, of "participation with Him even in this life!"

"He attains appeasement, he in whom all desires are engulfed as the waters are engulfed by the sea which grows full and yet remains immutable—but not he who desires his desires. The man who, stripped of all desires, marches without covetousness, without 'my' and 'I', will attain appeasement.

"This is the doctrine of Brahma... He who has acquired it will no longer lose his way. And if he possesses it in the final hour he will arrive at Extinction in Brahma."

The second epic, the *Ramayana,* "the verse-chronicle of Rama's heroic exploits", is attributed to Valmiki, who is said to have composed them by assembling the scattered elements of a long oral tradition.

A tale born in mythological times, it tells of the infancy and youth of the hero Rama, a king's son, and of his marriage with Princess Sita, "born from a furrow in the ground." He won her, like Arjuna in the *Mahabharata,* by bending a prodigious bow which his rivals could not even lift.

A man should have a favorite god, but he must also honor the gods of the home, the god of the village as well as the protecting genii. Before the sanctuary of the goddess Bajresri, the worshippers in the Kangra temple intone the hymns of salutation: "Let us make sacrifices to him who gives breath, who gives strength, who orders us to venerate all the brilliant gods, he whose shadow is immortality. Let us offer sacrifices to him by whose power the mountain and the sea exist... let us offer sacrifices to him by whom the sacred earth and sky were created and made solid, to him who established the air and the firmament..."

And here again the struggle is organized between Good and Evil. The jealousy of his father's favorite wife brings about Rama's exile to the forest. Sita implores him to permit her to go with him:

"If thou leavest now, descendant of Raghu (the Sun), for the impassible forest, I will walk before thee, crushing the thorns... Throw off, thus, envy and anger like the water which remains after one has drunk and lead me, hero, in all sureness! Nothing there will hurt me.

"Under the vaults of the palace, in chariots, in the wake of birds, wherever it falls, the shadow of a husband's feet takes precedence...

"I will go into the wayless forest, untrodden by man, filled with every sort of beast, inhabited by bands of tigers; I will live happily in the forest, as in my father's house, without concern for the three worlds, concerning myself only with the sole law of wife. Always obedient, dutiful, chaste, I will find my pleasure with you, hero, in the forest with its sweet fragrances."

When Rama refuses, pointing out the "unhappiness of life in the forest," she insists.

"Separated from thee, Rama, I would have to renounce living... If I were by your side, Indra himself... the master of the gods, could not attack me by force... O pure heart, my love will render me inaccessible to impurity: I will follow in the steps of my husband, for the husband is the supreme divinity. After death a blessed union will be given with thee forever... Any woman in this world who has been given by her parents to a man, whith ritual waters and according to his law, belongs to him in the other world as well, O magnanimous one."

Sita is finally allowed to accompany Rama to the forest, but the chief of the demons, Ravana, kidnaps her

"Do not try to measure the immeasurable with words, no more than to plunge the cord of thought into the unfathomable: he who asks is mistaken, he who answers is mistaken."
(Words of Buddha). An undated statue from southern India.

"Like a moonless night, like flowerless trees, such are the countries and regions deprived of the beneficial virtues of the Ganges. Like a sunless sky, an earth without mountains, an atmosphere without wind—thus undoubtedly are the countries and regions that the Ganges does not bathe. If the wind which has caressed the waves of the Ganges touches a man's skin, it immediately carries off all the sins he has committed. As small children tormented by hunger crowd around their mother begging, so men here below, desirous of attaining their salvation, hurry imploringly to the Ganges!"

Such are the virtues of the Ganges celebrated in the Mahabharata. Benares—formerly Kaci—Siva's luminous city—Benares, the oldest city in the world, is the junction, it is said, of the three Ganges: the celestial Ganges or Milky Way, the terrestial river, and the great undergound river which flows from the Himalaya.

by trickery and carries her off to his residence in Lanka (probably Ceylon). To deliver Sita, Rama becomes the ally of the "army of monkeys", led by Hanuman. He kills Ravana and, his exile ended, he returns triumphantly with Sita to Ayodhya (modern Oudh), capital of his kingdom. However, his jealousy begins to nag him, and he wonders if Sita was not unfaithful to him during her imprisonment. He repudiates her. She is prepared to be burned at the stake, but the god of fire spares her, attesting her innocence.

The *Ramayana* is surely the work that has enjoyed the most extraordinary circulation throughout India itself and in territories under Indian influence. It gave rise to a whole Rama-inspired literature, expressing itself especially in drama. Furthermore, it is found in all forms of art. It can be said that it favored, by the knowledge it gave of Rama and Sita,—models of the Indian soul—the establishment of a popular national cult, a sort of Raman religion.

Standing beside these great epics, and drawing its inspiration from them, is *Sakuntala,* the masterpiece of all Indian dramatic art written by Kalidasa, the greatest poet of classical India.

It is the very simple story of a king, who was led by the hunt into the depths of the forest. There he discovers a hermitage, where Sakuntala lives, falls in love with her and gives her his ring as a sign of recognition. Lost in her dream of love, she is cursed by an ascetic, whom she neglected to greet and loses the precious ring which alone could awaken the memory of the king.

When the first translation of *Sakuntala* reached the West in 1789, Goethe was full of admiration and sensed all that the great oriental texts could bring to the world.

And at the beginning of our century Apollinaire, the

N*othing can disturb the meditation of this "thinker of the forest" who has chosen as a retreat the hill where the sage Agastya meditated, near Cape Cormorin. Recognizable by his yellow suit, this Sadhu has voluntarily renounced his family, his caste, the goods of the world. Henceforth, he will consecrate his life to the search for union with* Brahman, *that absolute which is everything, to attain the release from* Samsara, *the endless round of existences.*

During spring celebration of the holi, all India is joyful. White clothing is splattered with colored liquids. The stranger is immediately welcomed by hundreds of smiles, revealing sparkling white teeth; his arrival sets off a lively saraband among the boys who will soon become his friends. The small children, however, are shy, as shown by this young fisherman taking refuge under his basket, and the mute questioning of the little bronze-faced girl.

French poet, again used the theme in his poem about the *Mal-Aimé*

> "The royal spouse of Sacontale
> Weary of victories, rejoices
> When he finds her paler
> From waiting and eyes pale from love,
> Petting her male gazelle."

★

But well before the 19th century's passionate interest in the Orient, which innaugurated a methodical study of the texts and their translation, Indian thought had slipped imperceptibly into Western thought.

Wasn't it the very popular *Pancatantra,* a collection of stories and fables in which animals play the principal roles, that inspired La Fontaine? But through such a cascade of translations that one could no longer perceive the Sanskrit origins!

The Indian incense floating over the works of La Fontaine is due particularly to his friendship with a great traveler, Bernier, who, sharing with him Madame de La Sablière's hospitality, daily sustained La Fontaine's curiosity about the Orient. Having returned from the Court of Aurengzeb, the most orthodox and cruelest of the Mongolian emperors, where Bernier had been his doctor for eight years, he brought back a Persian translation of the *Upanishads,* treatises on doctrinal knowledge. Furthermore, he had been able to find a very wise, "lettered" pandit, who was so desirous of learning the principles of Western biology and metaphysics that he had agreed to initiate Bernier, in return, into the "Brahmanic theology."

"You are the cloud and the rain and I am the peacock. You are the moon and I am the partridge. You are the lamp and I am the wick. You are the site of the pilgrimage and I am the pilgrim. You are the gold and I am the borax. You are the tree and I am the bird. You are the pool and I am the fish."

(A popular Indian song).

46

Thus "the authentic India behind the conquered India" was rediscovered, and the "partial humanism of the classics" was about to become "the integral humanism which now seems to us to be a product of nature."

★

If one can forgo a speedy arrival by plane into the heart of India, one can find the old maritime route of the East Indies; the very one that was discovered by Vasco da Gama at the end of the 15th century in the name of his King, Manuel of Portugal. On July 8, 1497, he left Lisbon at the head of four vessels manned by a crew of one hundred and sixty men. Driven by the favorable north wind, they put into port at the Cape Verde Islands, called at Saint Helena on November 4, and on November 22 passed the Cape of Good Hope. It was from there, after having repaired the damage incurred by the ships, they went on from the discoveries which Barthôlomeu Diaz had just made. Sailing to Mozambique, they anchored. Badly received, they left, and on Easter Sunday, 1498, entered the roadstead of Melinda on the eastern coast of Africa. The prince put them in the care of a skillful pilot, who led them towards the Indian shores: they reached Calicut in southwest India, on the Malabar Coast, towards the end of May. A little less than a year had gone by since their departure from Lisbon.

Vasco da Gama returned triumphantly to his country: he had assured glory for his king; wealth for his country in the commerce of cotton, precious stones and spices; and a new field of action for the missionaries.

In 1502 he returned to India and founded the Cochin Warehouse, south of Calicut. Almost until the

In Vishnu's temple in Kancipuram, the morning service, begun at dawn has just ended. A young Brahmin, punctuating his words with ritual gestures as he sits at the foot of columns in the stony presence of sculptured divinities, recites a few verses from a hymn taken from the sacred books of the Vedas. He recites from memory: even today the text of the Vedas is transmitted orally, from master to pupil, from guru to sichya.

In *Delhi* at sunset, young girls like to linger near the mausoleums that perpetuate the memory of the Lodi dynasty. The peddler has prepared their favorite delicacies. At the same hour in the country, the elegant silhouettes of women carrying large wicker-baskets on their heads stand out in the fading light of day.

end of 16th century, Portuguese establishments multiplied along the Indian coast. The principal one was Goa, in a fortified enclave.

However, annexed by Philip II of Spain in 1580, Portugal shared the consequences of the disaster of the "invincible" Armada in 1588. It was then obliged to fight for control of the Indian Ocean, which it had earlier succeeded in obtaining by monopolies from the Mongolian emperors.

Except for the radiant personality of a man like Saint Francis Xavier, the Portuguese had acted with such brutality that they facilitated the task of the Dutch, who were the first to try to take away their privileges.

They were closely followed by the English. In 1600 the English East Indian Company was founded by royal privilege. It bought up land on the coasts, and obtained the authorization to establish foreign trading stations and depots, whose security was protected by forts, in the manner of different European states. Present day Madras originated with the St. George Fort, in 1639.

In 1688 the Company was given Bombay by Charles II, a truly royal gift from the dowry of his wife, Catherine of Braganza.

Protected by the parliament which appointed its directors (at least until 1795, when, as a consequence of the stir created by the trial of Governor Warren Hastings before the House of Lords, this prerogative was given to the Crown in an effort to avoid choices guided by political rivalries), enriched by royal favor, freed of the French Company's competition by the Treaty of Paris in 1763, the English East India Company remained autonomous until the Act of 1858, which entrusted to a viceroy the administration of its possessions. These were considerable. The progressive decline of the Mongol

*A*lthough essentially religious, Hindu art exalts the human body. In all ages sculptors have accentuated the characteristics of feminine beauty: generous breasts and rounded hips enhanced by a sumptuous profusion of jewelry. On the sides of one of the sanctuary towers of the Osian temple, voluptuous scenes are crowned by exquisite stone lace.

empire had incited the Company either to annex or protect immense territories by maintaining the local sovereigns. It had established a policy of grandeur. "The idea spread that lordly behavior was necessary to acquire the Indians' respect." In reality, it "raised a barrier between the English colonial society, exalted as a superior essence, and the demeaned native society."

Burke, the father of the English liberal tradition, was indignant about the policies of the Company, and, during the Warren Hastings trial, compared it to a "State disguised as a merchant," and vehemently demanded its transfer to the Crown.

Too impassioned, perhaps, he was not heeded. It took the Great Mutiny of May, 1857, and the ensuing concern over the future of the English establishments to make the Crown decide to assume an empire of which Victoria was proclaimed Empress on January 1, 1877. Disraeli was in power.

The revolt of the three regiments of Sepoys, which marched on Delhi, took possession of it, and won over the victims of the most recent annexations in the Ganges and Yamuna valley and central India, finally ended in a consolidation of British domination.

It was carried out with an easy economy of means by the intermediary of the Indians themselves—headed by a very small number of Englishmen—if one considers the expanse of territory and the density of the population.

The important work of building roads and canals, the construction of railroads, undertaken during the government of Lord Dalhousie between 1846 and 1848, continued. They were to permit the now independent India to work at righting its economy, which had suffered severely from the great industrial revolution of the 19th century. Considered a reservoir of raw cotton, it

The Rathor dynasty reigns over Jodhpur, capital of Rajputana. For more than sixteen centuries these pure-blooded Rajputs have ruled the land won formerly in battle. The Rathor cenotaphs stand on the site where Jodha, in 1459, built the city which bears his name. The tombs of the ancient kings are protected by the imposing bulk of proud and monumental effigies. An enormous procession of painted figures, these personalities are not distinguished monarchs or members of the royal family, but simple citizens, national heroes, immortalized forever in the glory of their past exploits.

56

consented to develop its culture wherever practicable, even at the expense of food cultivation. In return, flooded with cotton manufactured by the factories in Manchester, it witnessed the ruin of its own working classes.

However, at the beginning of the 20th century, the initiative of national companies inaugurated a trend towards industrialization on Indian territory—prelude to Indian independence!

As for the French East India Company, it was born in 1664 under Colbert's influence. In 1770, Jacob de la Haye, at the head of a fine fleet, failed in his efforts to create a French establishment in Ceylon: the Dutch had just preceded him. He then returned to France, but left behind François Martin, who was granted Pondichery by the Mussulman sovereign, dissatisfied with the Dutch.

Pondichery had a strange destiny—seized by the Dutch in 1693, and by the English on four occasions during the 18th century, it was restored in 1788.

Tradition has it that Dupleix, heir to the title of nabab, conferred upon him by Governor Dumas, was prevented by his recall to Paris from assuring France the empire of the Indies. In payment for the protection he had given the Mussulman princes, he was, indeed, named governor of the southlands extending from the Krishna River to Cape Comorin "and believed himself to be the master of India." In reality, it was only the concession of a "fictitious gift founded on the decision of sovereigns without sovereignty."!

Thus the Treaty of Paris of 1763, which assured France the five trading companies, leaving the English a clear field, was merely the abandoning of a great hope.

★

The monsoon rains have filled the basins; the fisherman standing on his narrow raft throws out his revolving net. The temple of Tiruvannamalai—in the Tamul region—raises above the coconut trees the truncated pyramid of its tower. It is said that the mountain which dominates it was, in the dawn of time, a column of fire. Many pilgrims and tourists flock to the ascetic's hermitage.

Everywhere in southern India, colossal, polychrome figures in terra cotta loom up: protective heroes who are honored, or
has long been familiar with these personages, possessors of magic powers, and knows how to convince them to give their pro
are worn once a year for the great festival; the wooden statue of the monkey Hanuman flanks a processional chariot: the a

...that must be appeased by offerings. This young peasant ...ching harvest. Masks of the gods of Krishna-Attam ...s the gods down into the midst of men.

Towards the end of the 19th century, the cutting of the Isthmus of Suez—where since earliest times so many caravans had passed to transfer merchandise from the Mediterranean basin to the Red Sea—assured the reopening of the Mediterranean. Thus it is by this maritime route that one enters the Indian Ocean to reach Bombay through its immense natural harbor, that magnificent bay which at night sparkles with a thousand lights like a glittering necklace, symbol of the poetic India of legend.

Beyond the ships coming from the four corners of the earth, under a gray, overcast sky, the city slowly takes form with its square, modern constructions resembling miniature skyscrapers. Caught between the West and Asia the traveler is offered, first of all, as if to reassure him, views that remind him of Europe: wide avenues, tall, bright buildings, the comfort and luxury of a few large hotels, the architecture of the station, the University and administration buildings. But in the middle of this official Bombay—the English-style Bombay with its proper Christian temples without originality—the Indian crowd swarms, an extraordinarily compact crowd, part of a city of four million inhabitants.

The crowd is there, it is everywhere.

It is an army of coolies, dressed in orange, red, navy blue, with dark faces shining with perspiration. They crowd together in the port, in the station, unloading and transporting merchandise of such tremendous weights that their legs are bowed.

White crowds of people who work in offices or stores move along in such packed groups that they seem to be coming out of a meeting.

A grave crowd of men are dressed in black frock-coats buttoned up to the neck, and in narrow white trousers or in *dhotis*—a piece of white linen worn tightly around

There is scarcely a place in India that is not in some way associated with the great epics. Each year thousands of pilgrims go to the temple of Rameshvaram. On his return from Ceylon, Rama, the prince charming and hero of Ramayana, stopped here where the temple now stands. To obtain pardon for having vanquished and then killed the demon Ravana, he paid homage to the god Siva. The sides of the pool rise in noble stairways with wide steps and descend to the water's edge; no visitor leaves the temple without filling the palm of his hand with this pure and sacred water.

In all times the exhuberant richness of the country
hospitable population have drawn to the Kerala co
Levant, Arabian or Phoenician traders. There the
ginger and indigo; today tea grows on the hills. At
rest on the dunes. In the shadow of coconut trees,
abandoning their bamboo houses, enjoy the evenin
trees waving in the wind. Soon, when the North S
the lagoon, immenses plaices, observed by aquatic
tireless, nocturnal swimming.

of a
the
pper,
boats
nts,
alm
over
their

the waist, raised behind, between the legs, over which floats a short muslin tunic.

A crowd of graceful and harmonious women are draped in *saris* of silk or cotton, permitting an individual elegance in the skilful arrangement of the folds.

A crowd of servants along the hotels façades, squatting in front of every door, await remuneration for heaven knows what work!

There is crowd of poor, crippled or merely lazy beggars. But also there are those "who choose for religious reasons to subsist uniquely from alms" and who procure "good points" for those who help them. They are called "sadhus," that is, "the good." "They are almost naked, their bodies often completely covered with white ashes, or dressed in ochre garments, with long hair wrapped in a bun on top of their head or... hanging loose, the forhead marked with signs of their sect... carrying religious objects, beads, pikes, tridents... of shells or enormous nut shells in which they receive alms. Many practice terrible mortifications of the flesh, exposing themselves to the sun, lying on cacti or on beds of nails, anchylosing a limb by remaining indefinitely in an uncomfortable position, piercing their cheeks or tongue with knives or pins... these are vows they have made to master their bodies."

There is crowd of those who, permanently installed in the streets, sitting or squatting on the ground or on a bench, perform small services. Some, armed with a long stem, clean ears; others, with a short blade, cut fingernails and toenails. There are barbers, shoe repairers, fixers of diverse objects using dirty bits and pieces to do so. There are those who read palms or establish horoscopes, so useful in arranging marriages or founding hopes on the future of the newly born. The most sought-after is

C*elebrated in the month of October all over India, the* Dussehra *festival takes on a particular charm in the Kulu Valley. This holiday commemorates the victory of Rama over the demon Ravana, the triumph of good over evil. The Indian's liking for processions and demonstrations is well known. The multitude of flags lends this fair a special appearance: it is regarded as a sacred and beneficial act to carry the heavy, richly decorated palankeen where* Ragunuth Ji, *the local divinity, resides for the festivities. And so this joyous population of mountaineers crowds around the chariot, protected by the richly dressed priest—A moving proof of the extraordinary popularity the* Ramayana *epic has enjoyed for centuries, and the pleasure it gives millions of people for whom the purity of Rama and Sita has become the symbol of conjugal love.*

probably the scribe. He breaks the isolation caused by illiteracy. Reading letters, some coming from distant provinces, he writes a reply dictated by his client. Curiously, he does not charge the same fee for all correspondence: love letters are more expensive because they require a great number of adjectives, and adjectives are money!

Bombay is a city of contrasts. It must be sought out, and the hurried visitor who goes from the port or Victoria Station to the hotel quarter or to the lovely buildings on Malabar Hill, can miss it completely. However, the men and women one passes, draped in *saris* or *dhotis,* come out of those narrow, steep streets studded with red blotches of betel, but streets sanctified by the presence of humble temples and sacred ponds.

At night thousands of bodies stretch out on the ground, on the steps of shops, in window recesses or even in the streets, since most of the latter have no sidewalks. Wrapped in fabric that clings to their bodies and covers their heads like a shroud, men, women and children await the coming of dawn, unmindful of passing cars or of people who may strumble over them.

Don't think that the Indian crowd gives an impression of sadness. Expressions of joy are less exhuberant than in the Western world, but there is less worry or, if you prefer, more indifference. One rarely sees tense, worried faces. The sort of serenity taught by the Indian philosophy is reflected in the attitude of even the poorest. And the brilliant ornament of the sun completes that ennoblement of the human being which was begun by the slow spiritual deepening bequeathed by centuries.

★

Temples, pillared halls, frescoes, and votive images are lasting proof of the feverish activity of the men of the 16th century. The temple of Virabhadrasvamin in Lepakshi offers an example of an architectural style with decorative originality, though conforming to southern tradition. The square pillars supporting the ceilings are decorated with charming reliefs recalling legendary episodes. The entablature rests on abacuses composed of enormous, conventionalized stone flowers which have remained unfinished.

"If there is a paradise on earth,
Is it not here?
This is the inscription engraved on stone in golden letters in Delhi. How can one describe the splendors of "Mussulman Rome?" The palace arcades stand out against vast lawns; in Fort Rouge, which has remained the symbol of Mongolian power, the sun's rays, despite the tremendous thickness of the walls, trace a mosaic of light on the floor through the stone lace of the screens (18th century).

In all of India, the need to participate in common traditions is expressed not only in pilgramages to sacred places but also in numerous celebrations: moments of national joy throughout the year.

Their origins usually date back to a very distant past. Their significance sometimes assumes so religious a character that they are preceded by a period of fasting. Buddhists, Jains, Sikhs, Parsees, Christians and Mussulmen add their own rites.

The most famous, aside from the Holi which celebrates both love and the springtime, is the Divali, "the string of lights."

A celebration of the acts of grace lasts three days; it opens with the end of the harvest and marks the beginning of a new year. Those three days consist of illuminations. Thus in the most ingenious manner each one applies himself to creating a fairy-like scintillation. Even the humblest houses are whitened, decorated with stars of transparent paper, of bright colors, with an inner illumination. Candles flicker on balconies and on the ground in front of the houses. Myriads of small lamps with dancing flames, as if alive, are placed everywhere. In Benares they glitter along the banks of the Ganges, and are reflected in the sacred pools of every city.

However, what predispose the cities to such an atmosphere of a gigantic fair are the thousands of shops squeezed together along the streets. Strange stalls, like the booths in a village fair, but which are the city's permanent stores! Doorless, inviting, decorated with luminous garlands, lighted by oil or acetylene lamps, overflowing halfway into the street and straddling the gutter, they have on display all they have to offer: copper in every form of useful instrument, trays, strainers, tea-kettles, pots, cups, water buckets, and

A *tower of victory marking the implantation of Islam on Indian soil, the* Qutb Minar *has for seven centuries haughtily raised its immense stone column of harmonius simplicity. A belt of sculptured balconies is attached to it like the machicolations of a fortress. Clinging to the angles, or gadroons, of the wall, bas-reliefs unroll in long strips containing verses from The Koran.*

Each morning the
of their bodies has n
out of their bath the
leave to the chinking
far away, in the foa
stones worn by genera
is the object of attent
decorated for every

...he on the river's edge. The care they take
...anity but is a ritual ceremony. On coming
...i and braid or coil their long hair. They
...nclosed in their hollow ankle bracelets. Not
..., the dhobis beat clothes in rhythm on flat
...The elephant, symbol of force and wisdom,
... be born of a cloud, this animal is patiently
...hout. He resembles a monumental toy.

receptacles for unknown uses. Copper reigns here, and most tableware is made of it.

Close by the copper, the silver jewelry catches the women's eyes. Frequently it is the most modest who are the most heavily decorated. What a joy to embellish one's neck, arms, ankles with heavy necklaces or thick rings, to frame one's face with decorations sometimes so cumbersome that the hole in pierced ears has stretched to the size of a buttonhole! Toes are adorned with large rings. It is especially on the days of the Divali that these marvels are bought, that women's eyes sparkle with a desire to possess them.

Saris of long, unfolded silk create an atmosphere of richness and joy. All the Indian provinces participate in the display: the fragile silks from Benares, the wondrously soft fabrics from Cashmir, the shimmering beauty of those of Maisur. Precious fabrics are interwoven with threads of silver and gold, with sumptuous borders destined for important ceremonies and for the trousseau to put in the hope chest. But right next to them, for the poor, are somewhat stiff and compact fabrics, rough cotton prints from the different provinces.

Every woman looks, caresses, hesitates and then, with a happy smile, makes her choice.

Gold or colored sandals, embroidered or lacquered, are also very tempting.

There are large shawls, striped cotton rugs, and books are on display for the curious. Copper pots and rows of deep green leaves announce the preparation and sale of betel. The merchant cuts the leaves carefully and places a small portion of paste on each one. The smell of betel wafts everywhere. The people chew it conscientiously, spit with satisfaction; their reddened teeth, their scarlet tongues remind one of debonair dragons.

The most refined expression of architectural genius in northern India was freely treated in the 11th century on the walls of the temples of Khajuraho. Stone men and women impetuously embrace, intertwine, and unite, abandoning themselves only to find themselves still more united, offering the faithful their seductive sensuality. Let us leave aside the opposing schools of thought which seek in them an esoteric significance, and let us believe that never before has man's eyes been offered more esthetic witnesses of expressive gestures, of soft looks, of passionate moments, of gracious smiles.

Mixed with the acrid odor of betel is a scent of amber and incense that comes from sandalwood.

However, a smell of thick grease announces fritters being cooked in big black pans over small wood fires: piles of crepes, *chapattis,* pile up. Some are very sweet, others extremely spicy, flavored with curry and other seasonings. On copper trays one sees heaps of grilled rice, beans, and mounds of a sort of small, crusty-looking vermicelli, saffron in color, made with pea flour and spices. This is where the children congregate. Furthermore, these "sweets" of the Divali, a sort of ritual cake, appear to be, by their ingenious diversity, a real treat for young and old.

These small businesses extend for miles. All street intersections are full of them. More often than not these stores do not have a second floor for living quarters. One sleeps on a camp-bed, the famous Oriental bed, and lies down at night on the same white, flat eiderdown on which one has squatted all day. A few of the houses of the city which stand a little higher, built of light wood with an overhanging second story, are reminiscent of European houses of the Middle Ages. But they never have the gay appearance of the old quarters in Strasbourg, for example. Everything is gray and, although not sad, tinged with an Indian atmosphere, which has something passive and resigned about it.

Everyone has put on his best clothes, his holiday clothes. The women have drawn on their foreheads the purple sign of beauty. The part in their hair is accentuated by a reddish line as are the soles of their feet, in open sandals. They walk silently, carrying on their hip a little boy in tight white pants; a small, man's shirt shows beneath a short vest, usually in velvet decorated with gold or glass-beaded braid; while on their head they

Great caravans no longer cross India, going from China to Ceylon, from Assam to Iran. In our time, nomads go from village to village, transporting in their simples carts their hut and their worldly possessions. Occasional farm hands, bamboo pickers, magicians, they weave mats and make fans... This caravan has stopped near the river in Tirokoilur; the women are preparing the evening meal, the men talk and the animals rest... The tales of Hiuan Tsang, Marco Polo's Chinese pilgrim, are recalled in this country scene, a striking illustration of ancient times.

I*n his incarnar*
tender spouse of
the god Siva c
reason, is designa
tion has been c
*dancers of the *
as those sculptur

god, Vishnu remains the
ing to Hindu mythology,
and Nataraja, for this
nce." The artistic tradi-
d to our time, and the
yle adopt the same poses
ram temple.

wear a skull cap, embroidered and re-embroidered in gold and silver in a design vaguely reminiscent of the crown of the Holy Roman Germanic Empire. The little girls are also draped in saris, and their shining braids are interwoven with flowers. The men, almost all in white, talk a lot and make their way with difficulty along the road encumbered with pedlars offering the children sausage-shaped balloons, crawling paper fish, and a whole assortment of delicacies.

At every step you are offered small, finely cut-out copper plates, a sort of stencil on which one rubs chalk or colored powder, used for decorating the ground which has been swept clean of its eternal dust. In this way, *rangolis*, multicolored rosettes, are designed. Thousands of people take part in this occupation, for the feet of passers-by continually efface this naive enchantment.

Beggars harass you, especially women with a tiny baby clinging to her breast. They insist, pursue you, chirping tirelessly, touching their foreheads, their mouths, their stomachs, calling attention to the child, and if you enter a shop they wait patiently to continue their shrill mimicry when you come out.

It is difficult to imagine the extraordinary congestion of those narrow streets without sidewalks: the unbelievable human mob blocking the passage of bicycles, rickshaws, *tangas,* fragile carts drawn by an emaciated horse, heavy wagons drawn by oxen with gilded horns and hoofs, archaic buses, and cows bedecked in garlands of jasmin or red laurel with painted horns, their backs covered with multicolored shawls.

And yet the entire crowd is not in the street. On the second floor, in strange, overhanging windows, on verandahs, spectators crowd together to watch the scintillating bustle below.

The Indian temple is conceived as a representation of the Cosmos. In Kangra the tower that crowns the sanctuary symbolizes the mythical mountain where the divinity resides. The haughty Himalayas stand out in the background. Vanquished by man, their summits nontheless remain the dwelling place of the gods. At the foot of the Himalayas, nature develops in its majesty, creating a spectacle over which even the most blasé traveler becomes enthusiastic: it leaves an impression which lasts a lifetime, which nothing can efface or equal.

The Hindu templ
mountain, on the ri
and pilgrims flock t
miles to worship the
ascetics in the Hima
from Benares to R
The pilgrims respect

universe. Ceremonies take place in the forest, on the
...dow of a sacred tree. India's holy places are countless,
...he difficulties in reaching them; they walk hundreds of
...nd to receive his benediction. They pay homage to the
... far from the world. Each morning two white eagles fly
...ve from the priest's hand the host—the sacred paesom.
...where these masters of the sky have landed.

Naturally, the Divali, like all Indian celebrations, has a religious aspect. The temples are not forgotten, flowers are strewn all over the ground, garlands of fragrant flowers are wound around the columns. To assure themselves the favor of the divinity, shopkeepers turn to Lakshimi, patron saint of wealth; they pay him the homage of their account books, on which they gravely affix wax seals. These registers pile up in the shops, and each page must receive this ritual ceremony of consecration.

Thus the new year begins in a gentle and exhuberant atmosphere of joy, where the gods are invited to take part in human preoccupations!

Our narrow schooner moves away from the port of Bombay in the direction of the small, squat isles that seem to guard it and where the Elephanta grottoes share with those of Ellora—also situated in the Mahratta region, not far from Bombay—the most admirable displays of Indian sculpture.

Carved out of the rock, the great underground temples dedicated to Siva represent the mythological aspects of this god through his symbol of cosmic force, both creative and destructive.

The central square sanctuary, supported by the oppressive majesty of alignments of enormous pillars crowned by massive capitals, has four entrances located in the center of each side. Two divine guardians stand there to defend them.

Inside is found the austere *lingam,* symbol of masculine creative energy. It stands serenely in the deepest corner of the temple, constituting the vital center of the sacred cavern.

Before the snows cover the mountains and block the passes, cutting off all communications, the mountaineers of Kula celebrate the autumn holiday. In long processions, to the beating of drums, the mountain gods descend to the valley to receive the homage of the faithful. This is an occasion to trade and to sell, to discuss business. Kula, at the crossroads of the Himalayas, became the biggest market in northern India. One travels from Laddak, from Tibet, from the valleys or Lahaul, and Spiti to go to Yarkhand or descend to Punjab.

But suddenly, as one's eyes begin to grow accustomed to the semi-darkness, from one of the sanctuaries the three-headed bust of Siva looms up. He is represented as the Grand Master, the personification of the plenitude of the Absolute, embodying the three apparently contradictory aspects of existence: creation, conservation, and dissolution, which are "one and the same thing as to the origin, the significance and the term." The comprehension of this unity is the goal of Hindu wisdom.

For wisdom, the religion of India, accepts "ruin and the forms of death as grave notes in a cosmic symphony, whose formidable music is the paradoxical expression of supreme quietude and the silence of the Absolute."

According to Grousset (speaking of Siva's statue), "universal art has succeeded in few materializations of the Divine as powerful and also as balanced." He believes that it is "the greatest representation of the pantheistic god created by the hands of man." He concludes with poetic enthusiasm: "Never have the overflowing sap of life, the pride of a force superior to everything, the secret intoxication of the inner god of things been so serenely expressed."

Before leaving Elephanta, the bas-reliefs of the marriage of Siva and Parvati add a lighter note to the mood of magisterial splendor. With a reassuring but sovereign elegance, they seem to sing of "the instinct of love which perpetually creates life."

On leaving, one carries off like a treasure that key to Indian art found in the sculpture of the 6th century. Influenced by earlier Buddhistical art, it gives a foretaste of the later art to which it largely contributed.

In the sky, high above the Bombay roadstead, the slow and haunting circling of vultures watches over the towers of silence where the bodies of the Parsees are

The Himalayan inhabitants take an extremely lively part in their celebrations. Men and women from the Lahaul and Spiti valleys bring their innocent desire to amuse themselves and to parade about in their richest costumes, covered with jewels.

Rajputana is the country of fortresses. Here live the Rajputs, whose ancestors were kings. Each stone of the Jaisalmer citadel has a history. The sun door, caught between two tall walls, opens onto the fort's hidden areas; from the terraces the eye can take in the entire city, with its labyrinth of square, flat-roofed houses. The enormous cannon of the Uparkot fort, today a relic of the past, recalls the many sieges in the 16th century which its inhabitants had to endure. Massive bastions, ramparts bristling with towers, the royal palace of Jodhpur dominates the plain from the top of its rugged, rocky hill.

conserved in order that the religion of Zoroaster be accomplished.

But we are already thinking of Ellora and its admirable series of grottoes dedicated either to Buddhism, Sivaism or Jainism. A forest of columns supports, here too, the flat roofs eroded in the rock or Buddhistical vaults.

Sojourn of the gods of Indian mythology, and entirely excavated in the 8th century, the temple of Kailasa, borrowing its name from the Himalayan mountains, seems protected by the fluvial dieties which guard its doors. Its reliefs, which rise in tiers, covering entire walls, are full of turbulent and descriptive vigor; they constitute a veritable narration of the principal episodes in the two great Indian epics—the *Mahabharata* and the *Ramayana.*

Siva and Parvati are represented there, too, in the scene of the kiss, and also on Mount Kailasa when the demon Ravana "begins to make the mountain tremble to obtain Siva's intervention against Rama. Parvati, terrified, throws herself against her husband in a spontaneous and naive movement," which is very feminine. But Siva, with his toe, calms the mountain and crushes the titan.

The cycle of Siva in Ellora reaches its culmination in the form of Nataraja, the Cosmic Dancer, "symbol of superhuman lyricism by which... medieval India has expressed its heroic adhesion... to Joy, Pain and Universal Force."

The stone, as if malleable, expresses the frenetic rhythm of the body and multiple arms in the manifestation of eternal energy.

But this stone reassumes its tranquil force to achieve the extraordinary elephantomachy where "caryatids of the Universe," the elephants, appear to sustain it.

The cavern temple of Elephanta, near Bombay, is dedicated to Siva. He represents infinite power, which endlessly re-creates what it has destroyed; he is the supreme master, Mahadeva; wise men see in him the personification of Soma, the sacrificial elixir. Here, in the middle of a population of serene-faced statues, stands the colossal image of Mahadeva. One recognizes, by his triple visage, that the ancient Dravadian divinity embodies in his being all the powers of the other gods.

93

At *Mavalipuram*, on the Coromandel coast where the powerful Pallava dynasty reigned, not far from the monolithic temples, the rathas, *an immense bas-relief,* covers the granitic side of a cliff. The crucial episode represents the descent to earth of the purifying water of the celestial river, the Ganges. The nagas, personages with ophidian bodies, have traced the river's course in the rock, and all creatures hurry to honor it. Might not these animals, which participate in the general joy, be the ancestors of those that men are trying to protect in the Periyar reserve?

In the isolation of Ajanta, northeast of Ellora, a long succession of grottoes sheltered Buddhist monastic life from as early as the first centuries A.D.

Gradually transformed into an underground monastery, they open by a series of columns whose capitals recount the anterior lives of Buddha. They complement the reliefs covering the walls. The Buddha's stone legend is presided over by his seated effigy at the base of a stupa, which ends with his colossal statue, reclining in the attitude of the Parinirvana, "Extinction."

In these caverns of Ajanta is found the greatest collection of Buddhist paintings, owing to the piety of the faithful who, during several centuries, decorated the caverns with frescoes painted in the style of the Gupta dynasty. As a "materialization of the ideal vision of the Buddhas and the bodhisattvas, Ajanta is equal to Mathura and Sarnath... The Indian idyll and the flowering jungle that make up the background are there only to emphasize the figures of the bodhisattvas... Supernatural visions which number among the most moving that have ever been born of the human dream." The hands succeed "in expressing the almost Franciscan tenderness which animates them." They seem to accomplish "gestures coming from the soul," "it is pure moral beauty translated directly into esthetics."

However, the illustrations of the earlier lives of Buddha, which evoke the most poetic legends of his preceding existences, abandon a measure of idealism to attain "a more intense dramatic sense: it is a matter of a more direct art which speaks to the people."

And to know these people who long ago abandoned Buddhism, one travels miles through the Indian countryside in search of the places sanctified by that Blissful One.

One goes through crowded villages of mud-wall

The Kerala, land of the Malayalis in southern India, trembles from the uninterrupted beating of drums in spring. At that time all is dancing, music and joy. In front of the village temple, the Therayattam dancers, wearing immense headdresses of carved wood, come to honor the Dravidian divinities. Dances of extreme violence, in which men, in order to vanquish evil spirits, try to win the favors of some and exhort supernatural powers.

shanties, on which cow dung dries, making it combustible. Often, in the peace of the evening, one hears a song psalmodizing a monotonous prayer accompanied by a vina. Or else the village bard, the very one who knows by heart the genealogical tree of the local prominent people, organizes a recital of scenes from the *Ramayana* which lasts well into the night. One might also obtain permission to attend a wedding, always invested with great dignity, for the villagers, though often so poor, consent to spend a lot for the festivities and even more to assure their daughters a dowry of money or jewels. They go into debt for long years with pitiless money-lenders, but find consolation in a few hours of escape from their miserable lot in life.

But a more special aspect than all the scenes of daily life is found in the village of Rajaldesar in the Bikaner province, one night by train to the southwest of Delhi, where there is an amazing religious gathering: a Congress of Jain monks and nuns.

Like Buddhism, born in the 6th century B.C. and fragmented over the centuries, the Terepanthis sect that united in this Rajput town was the result of a reform which took place about two hundred years ago. This reform carries out in the most rigorous and unexpected manner—for us—the rules which are found in the Jain Canon. They may be summed up in five large injunctions. First of all, the observance of absolute non-violence, an idea consistent with Indian tradition but which takes, in Jain application, certain extremely curious forms. To avoid harming the life of any creature, however small it may be, the Terapanthes wear a small white rectangle over their mouths that is attached to their ears by a string, which prevents the swallowing of insects. Behind this screen they talk and sing, thus

98

In the days when our first cathedrals were being built, Belur was the flourishing capital of the Hoycala dynasty. A masterpiece of medieval art, the Chennakesava temple, dedicated to Vishnu, was erected in 1117 by the king Visnuvardana. On holidays it welcomes tourists in search of old, sculptured stones. Here, in Sunday garb, is a charming family; the father wants a souvenir of his visit so he photographs his little daughter in a niche which was formerly reserved for a goddess.

Bombay lives in a Western rythm: a business center, a cosmopolitan city with reddish buildings of colonial style, offices, banks, factories, and perpetually crowded streets. But the peaceful life of the humble remains controlled by shadow and sun. Here the Sikh merchant sits, tailor-fashion, in the midst of heaps of fruits; the barber accomodates his clients on doorsteps; the wool spinner keeps busy, but the shoe repairer, without work, dozes philosophically.

protecting the wind, a living element. However, at the hour of their sole daily meal, which is permitted only between eleven o'clock and sunset, they rearrange this contrivance a little. But in the evening one can see their white silhouettes gliding along, as if immaterial, as they wave in front of them a sort of long-fringed mop in order to brush aside all living creatures. Every day at the same hour, this instrument of peace with nature is carefully unrolled and shaked.

Having no right to use metal objects, they pull out their hair and beards with their fingers. For this operation, very young priests with abundant heads of hair seem to have to carry out a Sysyphean labor; they devote themselves to it after covering their head with ashes. However, these ashes are not taken from their fires, for they are forbidden to light one, fire being both a living substance and a destroyer of living matter. But all their food must be cooked and their water boiled, so they must obtain it as a gift; and without asking for it, since they are only permitted to sollicit bread and water. The rest, consisting exclusively of vegetables, can be accepted on the condition that the donors share it with them and do not prepare any food especially for them.

Lodged in houses richly decorated with gilding and enamel—the homes of patriachal-type families, which sometimes consist of as many as two hundred people— these seven hundred priests and nuns received the hospitality of an enthusiastic and mystic population that was almost entirely at their service. For this meeting they had walked barefoot for hundreds of miles without using any form of transportation, returning from places where, by groups of five, they had received the order to preach during the monsoon. To Rajaldesar, which has only a small railroad and sand trails, came thousands of pilgrims

In the pool of the Sikhs Temple of Gold in Amritsar, the men perform their ablutions while carrying on a lively conversation. A woman leaning on a tree waits for her sari to dry. One could say she is making the ancient gesture which assures fertility.

Statuesque, indifferent to the weight of the copper jugs filled with milk which crowns them, perhaps these dairy-maids of Somnath are thinking of the god Krishna who was, according to legend, incinerated here. An incarnation of Vishnu, he is the counsellor of Arjuna in the epic, but he remains the protector of shepherds, the companions of his youth. Somewhat of a prankster, he one day stole the dresses of the pretty shepherdesses bathing in the river and obliged them to come and get them, garbed only in their charms...

riding camels to join them, to meditate, listen and ask advice. On the day of the biggest ceremony, under an immense tent and sitting cross-legged on a high table, the high priest, called Acharya, a sort of pope, dominated a crowd of more than 10,000 followers squatting on the ground. He spoke untiringly, interlarding his speech with songs inspired by the advice and orders he was giving, all of which illustrated the Jain Canan. The songs in the Rajasthani language, the dialect of Bikaner, were repeated in chorus by the consecrated disciples, the Sadhus and the Sadhvis, and by a large part of the audience.

A calm and luminous joy animated the eyes of those men and women whose only personal possession is the thin white cloth that covers them. One felt that this life of morification, usually begun at eleven or twelve years of age, was for them not only acceptable but fervently desired.

It was a no less strange spectacle to attend the presentation of two little girls whose families implored their admission to the community.

Among the injunctions of the Jain Canon—if the laws against lying or stealing do not surprise us, and if the obligation to have no earthly possessions corresponds to the ideals of Western monastical orders—the rules concerning chastity astound us. It is forbidden to take a bath—and this in such a scorching climate that a bath or a shower is the only possible means of relief. The slightest contact with a member of the opposite sex demands thorough and painful purifications. When a very young boy tried to approach a group of nuns, the latter were thrown into unbelievable panic, pushing him away with a little broom and hopping frantically about to avoid any contact! A man and woman may not kneel

106

The guru Nanak, 1468-1538, a sort of Protestant Hindu, an Oriental Luther, aroused the Punjabs against the caste system and the adoration of idols. For three centuries the Sikhs fought the Moslems, Mongolians, and Afghans in defending Punjab, their land. Fanatics and heroes, they lived for that holy war and were the Indian rampart against Moslem tribes coming from the northwest. Under the protection of the great Ramjit Singh, in 1823, the Sikhs united: their capital was Lahore, but Amritsar has remained the religious city. It is both the Mecca and the Manchester of Punjab. The crowd is going to the temple. Coming through narrow, crowded streets, one emerges in a large square of white marble beside the black waters of the lake of immortality. The Temple of Gold—where the noble Book, the Sikh cannon, is venerated—is reflected in the water.

on the same carpet, and if a priest has a document to give to a nun or a laywoman he must place it on the ground or throw it to her, but never hand it to her.

This life of mortification does not have the same goal as in the Western world, a sort of mystic marriage with a definite god; rather, it is an effort to assure, as in Buddhism, extinction, that is, the certitude of deserving not to be born again.

To attain this Nirvana, religious suicide may be authorized. During the Congress, I was shown a thirty-year-old nun who had obtained permission to eat no more food. Lying on the ground, her hands open in a gesture of offering, I saw in her eyes the shadow that was beginning to cover them but which expressed a desire for voluntary sacrifice. About twenty Sadhus surrounded her, chanting Sanskrit verses.

Many of these Sadhus show great culture and an admirable knowledge of literature. Many are also gifted with great manual skill and create miniatures and illuminated manuscripts of great perfection; others weave and do intricate embroidery.

With childish joy they showed us their work, especially the coconut bowls that are so beautifully painted and decorated with verses written in an amazingly regular Devanagari.

The Terapanthes devote their lives to these tasks to attain inner peace for themselves and for those to whom they preach until the hour of Deliverance. When that day finally arrives, seated on a throne and carried aloft, the Sadhu, his mouth covered with a symbolic silver leaf, is taken to the funeral pyre amidst singing. In Rajaldesar we joined a procession that was both triumphal and funeral and which accompanied one of the monks who had used up his last strength to come to die among all his brothers.

Only four temples dedicated to the Sun God are found in India: in Martand, Kashmir; in Khajuraho; in Konarak; and in Modhera in Gurjat. The only vestige of the capital of the Solankis, the Modhera temple is oriented so that the sun, during the periods of equinox, illuminates its image through the sculptured pillars of the immense hall where bas-reliefs celebrate the glory of the god.

As soon as Krishna puts the magic flute to his lips, the dairy-maids' dance begins. In the courtyard of the Udaipur palace, a mystic dance is performed in a whirling of skirts. To learn the ritual gestures, codified by very ancient tradition, a long apprenticeship under the direction of a teacher is required. The make-up of the dancers of Kathakali demands hours of work. The spectacle often lasts all night. No words or songs are used; only the mimicry of the dancers permits one to recognize which episode of the Ramayana or the Mahabharata is being enacted.

"You were well aware, Shah Jahan, Emperor of the Indies, that life, youth, honor, and riches are swept away by time. And so you endeavored to make your agony survive the glories of the Emperor. The glittering strength of your sovereignty can disappear like the sparkle of the sunset behind the curtain of sleep; one small sigh from the soul can spread its color over the sky forever, for immense was your heart's desire. Yes, the splendor of gems and jewels can fade entirely away; tears shed one day will last forever, eternally pure, brilliant, limpid on the forehead of time, and this is the Taj Mahal. And this is the name which you gave to your Well-Beloved, in the solitary love of your temple, bathed in the moonlight. You have left that amorous murmer in the ear of eternity. The infinite delicacy of love blooms for you in the flowers on the heart of peaceful marble. And this was your marble dream: the Taj Mahal."

Thus, Rabindranath Tagore sang of the Taj Mahal, the mausoleum built in the 17th century, on a curve of the Yamuna River, in memory of his wife, Mumtaz Mahall.

The Congress over, the monks and nuns set out, always in groups of five, at nightfall to make the slow, arduous march to the many stages leading them to the place of their mission. The rich Jain merchants, on returning home, will try—not to renounce their wealth, for it is too great for them to have the courage to do that—but not to be greedy and not to steal! Their heads wrapped in multicolored turbans, and draped in cashmere shawls, they give themselves up to meditation, marked by the swaying of their camels in the night.

Passing from one village to the next, one reaches Sanchi. There, stupas are found that were perhaps built before the Christian era. Shrines in the form of tumuli, they cover the ashes of Buddha or the saints. According to legend, the pious emperor Asoka, in the third century B.C., initiated a search for the eight original stupas. Seven were found. He redistributed them throughout the empire and their number increased to eighty-four thousand!

The somewhat overwhelming massiveness of the great stypa of Sanchi is, in a way, corrected by stone balustrades which mark the boundaries of the sacred enclosure. They are embellished by very beautiful narrative statues that are also found on the tall proticoes which, at the four cardinal points, mark the entrances. Some attain the most detailed elegance, having benefited from the technique of the ivory workers.

In Sarnath, at the gates of Benares, the emperor Asoka, the servant of the *Dharma* ("the Law"), erected in the Park of the Gazelles where Buddha gave his first sermon, the famous pillar surmounted by three admirable lions. Originally destined to support the Wheel, symbol of the Law, they now seem to impassively assure its defense forever.

113

J aipur was found
century and becam
tana.   Seen her
meeting between ca
of the perforated
the Winds.   Ve
structures of the C
18th century by a
mical penchant, m
On the summit o
silhouette of the
former capital, sta
mosaics of the
summon up the ea

*jpu-
istic
front
e of
ange
the
ono-
ture.
cing
the
ering
to
ions.*

After following in the footsteps of Buddha, we return to the Ganges, the sacred Hindu river, "divine mother" of which Siva himself sings in a Puranas hymn: "source of redemption... The mountains of sins accumulated by a sinner during his million births are destroyed by simple contact with the wind laden with the Ganges' vapors... As fire consumes wood, so this river consumes the sins of the evil. Wise men climb the terraced banks of the Ganges... free from danger, riding in celestial chariots, ands go to Siva's dwelling. Sinners dying near the waters of the Ganges are delivered of their faults: they become the servants of Siva and dwell at his side. They are identical in form to him; they do not die—not even on the day of the total dissolution of the universe."

Thus, all along its banks, crowds throng, but particularly in Benares, the holy city, where many funeral pyres burn, bringing to the river the ashes of those who reached it before dying, to receive its benediction.

Symbol of cosmic waters coming to fecundate the earth, the Ganges is extolled in Mavalipuram, near Madras, on the coast of the Indian Ocean. An immense bas-relief (72 feet long and 24 feet high), one of the most beautiful and most dramatic perhaps of all times, describes the descent of the Ganges from heaven to earth. A gigantic cliff, looming up under the hot sun of southern India, has been converted into a "prodigious masterpiece swarming with gods, titans, genii, human beings and animals, all converging towards a large fissure... Undoubtedly, the cistern was filled for certain celebrations, and water came out of the crack like a waterfall which simulated the descent of a mountain torrent: the Ganges falling from heaven on the Himalayas, and then running down into the plain."

116

H*aving renounced the throne to which he was destined, in order to devote himself to an austere life, Siddharta, after six years of asceticism, gave himself over to meditation. It was in Bodh-Gaya that, seated in the shade of a pipal tree, he attained supreme knowledge and conceived his doctrine of salvation, triumphing over the attacks of the temptation of Mara, the god of death. Back in ancient times a temple was erected on the very place of the "Illumination," or the "Awakening." Generations of pilgrims from all corners of the world have contributed to its enlargement.*

Created in the 7th century, it gives material form to the myth sung of in the epic.

In Mavalipuram there are many artistic achievements. The intention of the Pallavas kings of southern India in the 7th century was to transform a rocky site into a multitude of small temples and vast sanctuaries, hollowed out of and sculptured in the rock.

Furthermore, each great dynasty multiplied the number of temples in its kingdom.

In the north they are massive, powerful, secured by rounded towers and vigorous arches thrusting up toward heaven, with pyramidal roofed porches formed of several recessed cornices. They are somewhat reminiscent of fortresses. In Orissa, where this architecture was maintained from the 8th to the 12th century, the temple of Lingaraja seems to preside over a site containing no less than several dozen others.

In the south the Dravidian temples are characterized by their enormous entrance towers, called *gopuras,* that have a pyramidal roof on which an exhuberance of sculpture begins and continues on the sanctuary roof—it, too, in the form of a pyramid—to such a degree that it seems to eat the stone! Thus appear, among so many others, the great temples of Sidambaram, Madura, Srirangam.

The Taj Mahal is often considered the most significant example of Indian art of the 17th century. A mausoleum of white marble in the midst of marvelous Persian gardens, it appears to be rather the artistic proof of Islamic conquest—but also the proof of the love of an inconsolable Mussulman emperor, Shah Jahn, for his dead wife.

★

In the courtyard of the great Tanjore temple, by a wall covered with inscriptions in Tamil, the Brahman medidates. "When a man is not conscious of his relationship with the world, he lives in a prison with walls hostile to him. When he finds the eternal spirit in all things, he is emancipated, for he then discovers the full meaning of the world in which he was born. In India men are enjoined to be fully conscious in their body and soul of the close relationship with all that surrounds them: they are taught to hail the morning sun, the water in streams, and the fertile earth as manifestations of that living truth which also embraces man...".

Who can say how many gods Hinduism ho
counting the stars in the sky. One comes to the
to one of the major figures of the Hindu panth
the protective divinity of one's choice. From the
ceremony, musicians call the devout, and the sh
drum. Music charms the gods, who will come
residence. Here is Siva, who dances in a ci
universe in motion; and Vishnu, who is carried
rests on the coils of a serpent, and floats

ult as
mage
lp of
igious
the
vorite
s the
ruda,
haos.

Hinduism "is not a religion like ours in the West, which could be defined negatively, at first, by isolating them from the whole of non-religious forms of existence. In some ways it is inseparable from philosophical speculation, and in other ways from social life. This social life is arranged within a framework of castes and is based on the idea of the "function" *(dharma)* of creatures and things, which designates, at the same time the Law in its widest sense, the order which presides over the facts in the normative disciplines, but more especially the moral law, religious merit: it is the only term which explains our word religion and which extends beyond and yet remains within."

Thus religion conditions every aspect of life. As for the vast pantheon of gods, it is only a mythological support, a succession of models which tradition transmits and which determines a certain behavior. Indian mystics have for long centuries attempted to attain the Absolute by the most complete renouncement.

India is above all the country of Buddhistic preaching, of the rigorous Jainist reform, which was also carried out in the 6th century B.C., pushing asceticism to its extreme limit. It is the land of "the teaching of the Vedas and the Upanishads, of the discourses of the Great Epic, of a whole treasury of maxims... which continue without interruption from the Buddhistic *suttas* (condensed phrases) to... Ramakrishna. It is the eternal foundation of Indian spirituality, it is India's reality."

"A deep-seated idea of mortification, of *tapas* or "ascetic burns," is inherent in Indian behavior. Gandhi's exaltation in an arduous life, his horror of luxury, his need to be poor... this is the echo of a whole past. It is by the severest self-discipline, such as classic yoga founded it, that the Indian hopes to find his way. To dominate

B*y poster, the population of Chamba has been invited to the annual performance of "Ramlila," but the last episodes of the life of Rama have taken place, and the joyous cavalcades no longer fill the streets. We must wait until next year to see them again. Will he still be there, this Mussulman patriarch who seems to guard the Hindu temple?*

*S*quatting in the hollow of a low Himalayan valley, Chamba's temples make strange silhouettes. Concerned with protecting their majestic cikharas from the snow and rain, the devout have given them roofs and porches. Behind the gold of the tiles, the peaks renew their grasp, and the view is one of a severe landscape. The slopes move towards invisible chasms, at the bottom of which churning waters roar. In the overwhelming beauty of the Himalayan forms, shepherds lead their flocks towards the valley; they have nothing to tell, except perhaps of some mountain drama. The solitude and grandeur of this place have lined their faces, as the wind and the rain and snow have sculptured the erratic boulders fallen from the peaks.

the natural instincts of the human being is one of the bases of his philosophy."

Gandhi "was above all the fortunate contact of a man with the latent aspirations of a nation." He was able to re-instill a magic force in the practices he employed.

Would his fasting, by which he created "only the menace of his own death," have had the same force in another country than India where, throughout the ages, the hunger strike has been a means of moral or religious constraint?

Ahimsa is not so much "non-violence" as "action founded on a refusal to harm"—"less non-fear than an active state beyond fear, for Gandhi taught the masses, exhausted by a long servitude, not to cease suffering but to cease fearing."

Isn't this what the Bhagavad-Gita teaches? Yet Gandhi admitted to having rediscovered its meaning back in 1893 in the Sermon on the Mount, which was for him the revelation of Passive Resistance! "A contemporary of dictatorships... in an age when the world was rent by passion, feeble and disconcerted," he triumphed.

One may remember the dialogue in which Malraux asked Nehru, "Since the Independence, what has been most difficult?" The reply was, "To create a just State with just means... Perhaps also to create a secular state in a religious country. Especially when its religion is not founded on a book of revealed religion."

For Nehru wanted India to be "promised to a unique destiny, devoted to becoming the conscience of the world."

126

Painted on the walls of southern India's temples, episodes of Sivan inspiration express in naive realism all aspects of life. Here is a series of allegorical scenes in which the principal divinity, provided with four arms, lays a set of traps for his devotees, testing their devotion which will determine their good or bad rebirth.

He refused to let this destiny take the form of *karma* (the whole ethical consquences of one's acts considered as fixing one's lot in a future existence) which would have to be allowed to operate passively. He wanted to "disenchant his nation. To show it how to draw on the past to find motives to believe in a renewal, not to find reasons for maintaining the structure which had caused decadence. Without disowning the values which gave India its prestige, he wanted to judge and dominate the social situation for which they were responsible."

Gandhi was deeply mystic, Nehru a rationalist. But their passionate love for India united them. And this love, for Nehru, could also find support in tradition, as is shown in his testament:

"Although I have rejected a great number of the traditions and customs of the past, although I greatly desire to see India throw off the shackles which hinder it, which repress it, which divide its people, which suffocate a great number and prevent the free development of body and mind... I do not wish, however, to make a complete break with the past. I am proud of this noble heritage which was and still is ours, and I am aware that I too, like all of us, am a link in that uninterrupted chain which finds its origins in the dawn of history, in India's immemorial past. That chain I do not want to break, for I cherish it and find my inspiration in it. It is in testimony of this and as a last homage to the cultural heritage of India that I request that a handful of my ashes be thrown in the Ganges at Allahbad, so that they may be borne to the vast ocean which beats on the shores of India."

I remember that distant day in 1948 when I saw him for the first time. It was at the home of the governor

In Malabar the streaming monsoon rains have ended, the new harvest has been garnered, and the sky has recovered its brilliant light. It is a time to celebrate during a whole week the festival of the monsoon. Girls dress up in their best finery, and houses are bedecked with flowers. One awaits the coming of Mahabali, the benevolent king with hands full of gifts. Who would miss the regattas at the vallomkali of Aramnulla? Here, on the Penriyar River, slender pirogues with serpentlike prows line up, loaded with hundreds of rowers; soon the paddles will beat the water in rhythm, in the rhythm of songs and drums.

Treated like human beings, animals occupy an important place in the Hindu pantheon. In northern villages, Hanuman, that demigod with a monkey's head, is venerated by all. Ganapati, Siva's son, represented as a man with an elephant's head, symbolizes intelligence. The white horse, Kalki's steed, the tenth incarnation of Vishnu, supports the god who, at the twilight of the present age, will come to punish the wicked, comfort the virtuous, and then destroy the world. The powerful bull, Nandin, Siva's mount, personifies the erotic instinct and justice. The cow is regarded with great respect; is it not the foster mother who attends all ceremonies?

"When I found myself face to face with nature in the Bengalese villages, my days were filled with joy," wrote the Bengalese poet Rabindranath Tagore in 1932, who sang so well of the beauties of his native land. On this endless moor, like a game of mirrors, massive temples of red brick pursue one another. The freshness and spontaneity of their curved forms with delicate decorations engraved in the brick, so similar to the thatched huts in the midst of bamboo and palms, recall the past. Djaya Deva came here to pray each day, drawing in this templed solitude the voluptuous sweetness of the verses of Gita Govinda, verses recalling the passionate love of Krishna the Beloved and Rada, songs still sung today in all of India.

of Bengal, in Calcutta. He came over and sat at my feet in Indian fashion. When I remarked on this simplicity, so unexpected in a prime minister, he smiled, saying, "Ministers in France are not accustomed either to standing on their heads like a yogi!"

Now Nehru is gone. But India continues to amaze us, to transmit its message of culture and spirituality. It is purusing its destiny and struggling to become a great modern state. On a parallel with its plan for alimentary autonomy through better irrigation, by the distribution of fertilizer and by the use of intensive farming methods, it is working to become an industrial country. Railroads, naval and aviation yards, and large dams are being developed. Steelworks and oil refineries are increasing in number. Nuclear centers are being built, and atomic research carried out by Indian scientists has already attained remarkable achievements. In 1961, Nehru declared that energy was the "symbol of almost all forms of progress," and hoped that India would use it for peaceful purposes.

Today India has chosen for its leader Indira Gandhi, who stubbornly labors to triumph over all difficulties, all incomprehensions, with typical Indian patience. For, as Nehru said to me with that strange smile, at the same time gentle, energetic and a little anxious, as if pursuing an inner dream, "India is a great country!"

Marie-Simone RENOU.

THE GREAT HOURS IN INDIA'S HISTORY

1000 – 2500 B. C.

Zenith and decline of the civilization of the Indus Valley whose capitals were Mohenjo-Daro (Sindh) and Harappa (Punjab).
The population of the Indus Valley practiced most of the industrial techniques of Antiquity : the weaving of cotton and wool, metalworking (copper, bronze, gold, silver), the cutting of semi-precious stones (jade, cornelian, azurite), painted and varnished pottery, porcelain. The women wore bracelets and necklaces. Common tools were hachets, hammers, razors, mirrors of copper or bronze, needles and combs of shell or ivory. The writing existing on engraved seals has not been deciphered.

1500 – 1000 B. C.

The northwest of India is invaded by the Aryans, a nomadic population from Central Asia.
The Rig Veda which contains the most ancient of sacred Hindu hymns is composed.

1000 - 500 B. C.

The Deccan civilization attested by the site of Brahmagiri near the present day Mysore (or Maisur) and that of Adichanallur in the extreme south of the peninsula.
The Aryans extend their conquests to Bihar and Bengal. The Magadha empire is established in the northeast.
The Vedas, the Brahmans and the Upanishads are composed. Birth of Buddha, founder of Buddhism, and Mahavira, founder of Jainism in the north of India.

500 - 300 B. C.

The northwest of India is under the control of Darius of Persia. Alexander the Great arrives in India (326).

300 - 200 B. C.

Chandragupta Maurya founds the first great Indian empire. Zenith of Buddhism.
Composition of the Arthasastra, the oldest Indian treaty on the theory of government, attributed to Chanakya Kautilya, Chandragupta's minister.
Megasthene, Ambassador of Seleucos in Chandragupta's court, writes *Indika*, one of the first accounts on India.
Zenith of the Maurya Empire under the enlightened reign of Asoka (264-227), grandson of Chandragupta.
Asoka is converted to Buddhism and has his law engraved on stone pillars in various provinces of the empire.
The Buddhist Council of Pataliputra, capital of the Maurya empire, organizes missionary activities throughout India.

200 B. C. - 100 A. D.

Implantation of Greco-Macedonian dynasties on the territory of the ancient Persian empire and in the north of India (Punjab and the Indus Valley).
The first versions of the two great Indian epics, *Mahabharata* and *Ramayana* are known. The *Bhagavad-Gita* is composed.
Invasion of the Parthians coming from Persia, then of the Scythians coming from Bactria.

100 - 300

Invasion of the Kushians coming from Central Asia.
Reign of Kanishka. The great era of expansion of Indian culture, Sanskrit and Buddhistic.
Composition of the famous Indian code of law, The Laws of Manou.
The first images of Buddha are sculptured by the schools of Gandhara and Mathura.

300 - 400

In the south of India, flourishing kingdoms in Andhra and Tamil Nad : Satavadhans, Pandya, Chola, Kerala and Pallava.
Development of an abundant poetic literature, called the cycle of the Sangam.
Chandragupta I reigns in Magadha and founds the Gupta empire (320). Mural paintings in the grottoes of Ajanta and Ellora.
Invention of the decimal system by an Indian mathematician.

400 - 500

Reign of Chandragupta II.
The golden age of classical civilization, assured by the victories, security, material prosperity. Sanskrit literature multiplies poetic works as well as theatrical and didactic; Indian science is at its peak.
Fa-hsien, a Buddhistic Chinese voyager, writes of his visit to the Guptan court.
Works of the great poet and dramatist Kalidasa.
The Hephtalite Huns attack the Gupta empire.
The oral traditions of the Jains are codified.
Foundation of the great Buddhistic monastery of Nalanda.

500 - 600

King Harsha of Kanauj restores the culture of northern India.
The Chinese pilgrim Huan-tsang describes the court of Harsha.
The Chalukyas establish their sovereignty over Deccan for 500 years.
Birth of the Rajput kingdoms in the north.

700 - 900

Arrival of the Mussulmen. Conquest of Sind by the Arabs.
Buddhism extends to Nepal and Tibet.
The Pala dynasty is installed in Bihar and Bengal.
Construction of the temples of Bhuvaneshvar.
The philosopher Shankara writes a commentary on the Upanishads.

900 - 1000

The Turk, Mahmud of Ghazni, attacks India, conquors Punjab and annexes the Arab kingdom of Sindh.
The philosopher Ramanuja teaches devotion to the gods.
Mohammed of Ghur and his successors take away Mahmud's possessions and overthrow the Rajputs.

1200 - 1300

The reign of Iltutmish (1210-1235) establishes on solid bases the sultanate of Delhi, the first Moslem state of India.
Construction of the temple of Konarak.
The Delhi sultanate spreads its domination to the south of India.
Marco Polo visits India.

1300 - 1400

The Vijayanagar establishes itself in southern India.
Lalla, Kashmirian poetess, composes her songs dedicated to Siva.

1400 - 1500

Tamerlan invades northern India and pillages Delhi.
Kabir, in his poems, demands social and religious reforms.
Birth of Nanak, founder of Sikhism.
Vasco da Gama lands at Calicut in search of spices.

1500 - 1600

The Portuguese establish a trading company in Goa.
Babur, founder of the Mogul dynasty, conquers India from Punjab to the Bengalese frontiers.
Saint Francis Xavier carries out his mission in India.
Reign of Akbar, the greatest of Mogul emperors, who brings peace and unity to northern India and conquers a part of Deccan.
Mirabai, the Rajputan poetess, composes her poems to the glory of Krishna.
Flowering of Indo-Mussulman art : mosques, tombs, gardens, portraits and miniatures.

1600 - 1700

The English East Indies Company is created.
The Dutch East Indies Company is installed.
Reign of the Mogul emperor Shah Jahan.
Tulsidas of Benares translates *Ramayana* into Hindu.
The Taj Mahal, jewel of Mogul architecture, is built.
Reign of Aurangzeb : constant wars for the conquest of Deccan.
The Dutch and English increase the number of trading stations.
The French Company of the East Indies settles in Pondichery.

1700 - 1800

Fall of the Mogul Empire.
The Mahrate Empire takes the place of the Mogul Empire.
Struggle for supremacy between the French and the English.
The English defeat the French : Clive's victory at Plassey (1757) and capitulation of Lally at Pondichery (1761).
The Treaty of Paris (1763) reestablishing peace between France and England recognizes the maritime and colonial victory of the English in India. France recuperates five trading stations : Pondichery, Karikal, Mahe, Yanaon, Chandernagor and a few other stations having a commercial interest.
Resistance of several Indian States to English domination : the Mahrate Empire, the Maissur, the State of Haiderabad.

1800 - 1900

The Wellesley offensive : England becomes the master of India.
Insurrection of 1857 : first manifestation of the struggle for independence.
The Indian nation becomes aware of itself.
Creation of the Brahmo Samaj Movement by Ram Mohan Roy in 1828; creation of the Prarthana Samaj Movement by Keshab Chandra Sen in 1867; creation of the Arya Samaj Movement by Swami Dayananda Saraswati (1824-1883).
The experiment lived by Ramakrishna Paramahamsa (1836-1886). Swami Vivekananda (1863-1902) reveals Ramakrishna's message at the « Parliament of Religions », held in Chicago in 1893 and creates the Ramakrishna Mission.
The Theosophical Society establishes its headquarters in Adyar, a suburb of Madras, in 1886; Mme Annie Besant's action (1847-1933).
Appearance of several movements for reforms as of 1876 : Indian National Conference (1883); Indian National Congress (1885).

1900 - 1950

The partition of Bengal in 1905 marks the rupture between the Indians and the British.
The racial tendency wins out in a meeting of the Congress in Calcutta in 1906. For the first time, the program of Svaraj (an autonomous government of India under British suzerainty) is adopted.
Gandhi leads the national movement in 1915.
England accords a Constitution by the *Government of India Act*, in 1919.
Round Table Conferences (1930-31).
New statute of federal character for India : the Constitution of 1935.
Mass action decided by Congress on August 8, 1942 against cooperation in the war.
Subhas Chandra Bose (1897-1945) leaves India to organize the armed struggle.
India becomes independent on the night of August 14-15, 1947, at midnight.
On January 30, 1948, Mahatma Gandhi is assassinated by a fanatic.
On January 26, 1950, India votes a new constitution and becomes a Republic.

TABLE OF ILLUSTRATIONS

138

PRINTED IN FRANCE THE 15th OF MARCH 1969
THE HELIOGRAVURE WAS PRINTED BY BRAUN
OF MULHOUSE AND THE ILLUSTRATIONS
IN COLOR BY DRAEGER OF PARIS

PHOTOGRAPHS BY **JEAN-LOUIS NOU** with the exception of: pages 72 - 94 - 100 - 110b - 112 - 114: **ARPAD ELFER.** - COVER IV - pages 17 - 107 - 117: **EVERTS-RAPHO.** - pages 70 - 92 - 102: **TÉRRIER-HOLMES-LEBEL.**